Ease Your Anxiety

How to Gain Confidence,
Emotional Strength And Inner Peace

Ease Your Anxiety

How to Gain Confidence,
Emotional Strength And Inner Peace

DR. JOAN I. ROSENBERG

Ease Your Anxiety © 2016 by Dr. Joan I Rosenberg

For information and request for permission, please contact me.

Email: DrJKeynotes@gmail.com

Tel: +1 (310) 876-2324

Web: www.DrJoanRosenberg.com

FREE RESOURCES
You can download and print copies of the exercises in this book.

Simply visit:

http://www.AnxietyFree.Space

DOWNLOAD FREE AND LISTEN TO

THE MINDSTREAM PODCAST
https://geo.itunes.apple.com/us/podcast/the-mindstream-podcast/id1034587865?mt=2

TABLE OF CONTENTS

Acknowledgements

To the one who not only models, but embodies kindness and what it means to age with grace, beauty and poise. An inspiration to all she meets... that would be my Mom. You make me want to be better with each passing day.

To my friends and mastermind partners. Your belief in me, and your support of me touches my heart more deeply than you can ever imagine. You inspire me on a daily basis. I love you.

To John Assaraf, Mary Morrissey, Brendon Burchard, Bo Eason, Pam Hendrickson, Mike Koenigs, JJ Virgin, Zemira Jones and Dr. Dan Siegel. For your belief in me, your extended hand and opportunities that allowed me to be part of vistas I once looked at from a distance. Thank you for your inspiration, belief and opening doors leading beyond the invisible boundary.

And to my exceptional clients, students, colleagues and friends. I am blessed by our connection and grateful for all that you have given and that we share.

And to everyone else I may have forgotten to give thanks and praise. I love supporting and serving you. You are my big why and it's a deep and profound experience to share in your personal and business unfolding, growth and transformation.

Disclaimer

The ideas discussed within this book represent the opinion of Dr. Joan Rosenberg, based on her years of study, teaching graduate psychology and conducting psychotherapy. The information and material provided within this book is for educational purposes only and the ideas are not intended to replace the advice of your physician, psychiatrist, psychologist, therapist, coach or mental health provider. You are encouraged to seek advice from a competent medical or mental health professional regarding the applicability of any idea with regard to your unique concerns, symptoms or condition.

The author of this book does not dispense medical advice or prescribe the use of any technique as a form of treatment for physical, emotional, or medical problems without the advice of a physician or psychologist, directly or indirectly. The intent of the author is only to offer information to help you in your quest for emotional well-being. In the event you use any of the information in this book for yourself, the author and publisher assume no responsibility for your actions.

The stories and results shared within this book are personal to the users only and should not be considered typical. As in any endeavor, you are responsible for your results and they depend entirely upon your self-awareness, motivation, practice and self-responsibility. As such, the information and recommendations provided in this book are here for educational purposes only.

Preface

Welcome to Ease Your Anxiety.

This represents nearly 30 years of hard work, experience and the wisdom gleaned from my incredible clients, students, seminar and workshop attendees. Maybe you are one of them!

I wanted to take a moment to share some thoughts with you about what to expect in this book.

First, it's interactive. There are several opportunities for you to go deeper in the content and also to gain access to more training.

Second, this book is for your growth and understanding. It's intended to help you think about changes that are possible and provide you with the education that allows you to make the types of informed choices that can lead to greater transformation. Have a journal or digital screen nearby to capture your ideas.

Third, it's for implementers. You'll see there's LOTS of ideas that you can use to grow. If you're the type who's looking for someone else to do the work, I regret, this isn't the book for you.

Fourth, this book is designed to start a conversation with you, give us a chance to get to know each other better, develop trust, a bond and ultimately help us decide if we will work together someday.

Fifth, this is a book that's packed with content and lots of ideas that you can implement if you wish. My intention and the purpose of this book is to show you possibilities as they relate to diminishing your anxiety. The upside – an opportunity to go after what most of us want – better relationships and the freer, more full expression of ourselves, the ability to pursue what gives us meaning and what we want.

I want to help you add value to your life and everyone you come in contact with. You'll notice there are opportunities in this book to register and access more training and YES, I do and will have some other great information products I'd like you to invest in because they work and I believe you'll have a better life with them.

If you like what you read, or most of what you read, I'd absolutely love to hear from you, get to know you better and find out what you learned - or better yet, post a picture on my facebook wall at http://www.facebook.com/Dr-Joan-Rosenberg or Tweet me @DrJoanRosenberg.

The BEST way to start a relationship with me will be to visit the web link below, watch or listen to the free training, and learn more about how you can increase your confidence, have more emotional strength and experience greater inner peace.

I look forward to getting to know you better!

Sincerely,

Dr. Joan Rosenberg in Los Angeles, California, USA.

DOWNLOAD FREE AND LISTEN TO

THE MINDSTREAM PODCAST
https://geo.itunes.apple.com/us/podcast/the-mindstream-podcast/id1034587865?mt=2

Introduction

What if you could really get a handle on the anxiety you experience on a day-to-day basis so it was only occasional or barely noticeable? How would that change your life? What do you avoid because of the anxiety you feel? What would you do differently if you experienced far fewer worries or your anxiety was so significantly diminished that you lived each day with much greater ease?

Anxiety is rough! It conjures up danger and pain, whether it is physical or emotional. Not only are you tempted to give in to it, anxiety sure can take a lot out of you. Wearing you out either through constant worry about things you said or did in the past or what you believe you may have to face in the future. Your worries may involve: concerns over the safety and well being of your partner, spouse, child or children; going to work and having to deal with an angry and explosive boss or a co-worker with whom you disagree; too many demands and unreasonable deadlines; people that you think are talking about you behind your back; or difficulty speaking up to offer a suggestion, share your opinion, ask a question, or clarify a request.

Perhaps you experience anxiety or worry about the future that involves your sense of safety and security, including touching on issues such as access to clean air and water or the purity of our food. Maybe you worry about physical safety that has to do with fires, floods, tornadoes, hurricanes, earthquakes or any type of violent crime. Our worries can be heightened by random and senseless acts of violence that punctuate our daily lives and routines. This list could go on and on. Clearly we live in unpredictable and uncertain times.

And, it's not like these worries go away, instead they actually interfere with your everyday activities and drain your ability to enjoy life. Thoughts that seem to loop over and over with no end in sight is downright exhausting.

The thoughts running through your mind are bad enough, yet you have to face all the bodily discomfort that comes with feeling anxious on top of those worries. That may include feeling agitated, jittery, keyed up or on edge; restless or easily fatigued; having difficulty concentrating or your mind going blank; irritability; muscle tension; and disturbed sleep, whether it is trouble falling asleep or staying asleep. Perhaps you experience sweating or stomach distress in the form of pain, nausea or butterflies. All of these symptoms are associated with anxiety.

ANXIETY AND BODILY SENSATIONS

☐ Feeling agitated, jittery, keyed up or on edge

☐ Restless or easily fatigued

☐ Having difficulty concentrating or your mind going blank

☐ Irritability

☐ Muscle tension

☐ Disturbed sleep whether it is trouble falling asleep or staying asleep

☐ Sweating

☐ Stomach distress in the form of pain, nausea or butterflies

Your anxiety and worry need not emotionally paralyze you nor prevent you from pursuing your goals and the life you dream about. It doesn't have to contribute any longer to the procrastination that stops you from getting stuff done and it doesn't have to maintain your habit of avoiding people, events or activities that interest you. It can be frustrating to think about all the social activities you have missed because of feeling flooded by worry and concerns about being judged by others. You can begin to change your experience right now by learning, understanding and using new strategies to handle your anxiety.

If you know anything about cognitive psychology, then you know that to reframe something means to look at it from a different perspective. And that's the goal – to help you understand worry and anxiety from entirely new perspectives.

Anxiety can be experienced in many different ways though the focus here is on what psychology and psychiatry more commonly describe as *'generalized anxiety'*. This type of anxiety involves multiple worries (e.g., how you might say the wrong thing, do something out of order, or anticipate that some event might go terribly wrong – and your worry is about a variety of different life events and situations). It could be about getting to work safely, or whether: you'll hit traffic or be late to work; the restaurant will prepare your food the way you like; the lines at the movie will be too long; your out-of-town guests will like your home, feel comfortable within it or enjoy their visit with you. You can generate an endless array of worries about any or multiple life events.

Think of worry anxiety as internally generated stress, as Dr. Bruce Lipton, a stem cell biologist, speaks about in his book *The Biology of Belief*. He describes the effects of such stress and the consequence of disease that follows, so being able to manage worry anxiety is very beneficial to your overall sense of well-being.

Events, issues and experiences involving past or recent trauma can be quite complex. Though you may find many of the suggestions helpful, the focus here is not on the type of anxiety linked with tragedies, traumas or post-traumatic stress. Nor is the focus on fear or on "hard-wired" fight / flight / freeze / faint reactions that occur in response to danger and life threat. The information contained here is intended to help you learn only about anxiety of the 'worrying-kind'.

If your worry and anxiety are more general in nature or involve concerns with what others may think of you (often tied to social anxiety), then you will find several ideas that may help diminish your concerns about being judged. If you face challenges with what is known as social anxiety, you may find the *Projection Correction*^{TM} exercise useful for you. It's at the end of this book.

How to Use this Book

While some ideas discussed here have the potential of shifting your experience of anxiety almost immediately, there are others that will require repetition. People differ on the length of time it takes to engrain a habit, ranging anywhere from 21 to 66 days and there is other information that suggests it takes approximately 90 days before neuroscientists can detect new neuronal growth in the brain. That means that some of these ideas will take mental practice – not once or twice – but countless times over. Many times each day and over many days. As you practice, please consider journaling about your reactions and insights. It is well known that writing helps embed such learning.

So let's agree that you won't give up and throw in the towel after just a couple times or a couple days of implementing a new idea. Instead, please agree to stay with the new practice for a minimum implementation period of 66 to 90 days. Many times each day. Many days. (See, I'm already practicing.) Will you make a commitment to do that?

Remember, the information and material provided within this book is for educational purposes only and any recommendations are not intended to replace the advice of your respective physician, psychiatrist, psychologist, therapist, coach or mental health provider. If you are receiving such assistance, you are encouraged to consult with that medical or mental health professional about the applicability of any idea with regard to your unique concerns, symptoms or condition.

Remember to let me know how things are going for you at:

Twitter: @DrJoanRosenberg and
http://www.twitter.com/DrJoanRosenberg

Or at

http://www.facebook.com/Dr-Joan-Rosenberg

Differentiating Fear and Anxiety

Fear involves physiological, behavioral and emotional responses to a _specific danger_... fear is adaptive when there is _a real threat_ and your bodily reaction is one that signals you to escape or avoid that threat. A response to fear is considered maladaptive when you have that same bodily reaction to escape or avoid but there is no real threat. Riding in elevators, going over bridges, being in a crowd of people, being scared of insects, bugs or spiders are examples of common fears.

Understand your response to fear as something that is innate – if there is a genuine danger or threat present, then you're going to experience built-in feelings and reactions that are neurobiologically 'hard-wired' into you. Start by noticing what is happening around you. Is there a real threat? Is there a clear and present danger? Is it happening now? Or very soon? Well, then you should be having the reactions you have (fight, flight, freeze, faint)... and it means your body's response system is working properly.

Often, however, people experience the fight–flight reaction at the wrong time... meaning that the stress reaction is happening when there is no real object of fear present. In this case, the person's response to fear is maladaptive. You can think of this maladaptive response as having the 'right reaction at the wrong time'.

Anxiety, on the other hand, is a diffuse sense of apprehension about some aversive event in the future that people believe they cannot control – so **fear** is distinguished from anxiety in that _**anxiety** is characterized by the expectation of a diffuse distress / danger in the future and **fear** is characterized by a clear and specific danger right now._

Fear is characterized by
a clear and specific danger right now.
Anxiety is characterized by the expectation of
distress or danger in the future.

Anxiety and Mastery over the Future

In psychology circles, sometimes anxiety is called the *"memory for the future"* – mostly because of the way our brain functions. The brain is both an associational organ and an anticipation organ.

Here's how it works. Your mind searches the past (finding an old memory, an association to something you already experienced or something you already know) to help you anticipate or predict how things will go in the future.

Though worry or anxiety may be linked with future situations or events, consider the possibility that your worries and anxiety is really about experiencing and handling unpleasant feelings you are presently experiencing... in other words:

When people experience anxiety, they are trying to achieve mastery right now over a feeling that they anticipate might happen in the future.

Let's see if that idea relates to you.

Are you frequently anxious?

Do you worry a lot?

What do you worry about, specifically?

Write those thoughts below:

1.

2.

3.

4.

5.

.

Stop and reflect on that idea for a few moments... *are you trying to achieve mastery right now over a feeling you anticipate happening in the future?* Keep in mind the thoughts you wrote down, then ask yourself, *"what feeling or feelings would I rather not feel that I am actively preparing myself to experience later?"*

Note those feelings here:

1.

2.

3.

I worked with Stephanie, a 22 year-old woman who conjured up countless possible disappointing scenarios as a way to have mastery over any potential disappointed feeling she might experience in the future. She would literally think up events that had to do with experiencing disappointment in the future, then she would run them over and over through her mind until she would see herself figure out how to handle the future disappointment.

Her future focused thinking, regardless of the nature of her imaginings, kept her out of being fully present in her life in the moment, and she was not facing whatever disappointments truly existed for her already. She stopped creating future oriented scenarios involving disappointment as she became more adept and capable of handling the disappointments she experienced in her everyday life.

> *Anxiety is an attempt to have mastery over*
> *a feeling, or feelings that have not yet occurred.*

Breathe Deeply and Slowly

If you do something similar, start by taking some **deep breaths** and refocus to the present and notice **WHAT IS** happening right now so you can feel more centered and calm. Remind yourself that you have experienced many of the feelings before (like sadness or anger) that you are worrying about experiencing in the future. Just having the knowledge that you've handled these unpleasant feelings before can help you believe that you have the emotional resources to cope with future unpleasant experiences. Begin to trust that you will be able figure out the other resources you'll need to handle the situation(s) about which you are concerned.

> *Take deep breaths.*
> *Stay focused on the present to*
> *remain centered and calm.*

I recently coached a man in his early twenties who complained of heightened anxiety and an inability to relax throughout each day. He described feeling edgy, that he was shaky, couldn't sit still and found that he had to constantly move.

Fast, shallow breathing contributes to the experience of anxiety, so he started with changing his breathing pattern from fast shallow breathing (which often feels located in the upper chest) to deep, slow breathing all the way to the base of his diaphragm. He used a 6 count inhale, 4 counts to hold his breath and then a 6 count exhale to slow himself down. He felt much more relaxed after 15-20 of these breathing cycles and he continued to breathe in this manner the whole time we talked. He has consistently used this breathing approach everywhere he goes – while driving, walking to class, playing cards with his buddies and studying, especially since no one notices what he is doing. His long-standing edginess and need to move all the time has entirely dissipated.

> *It's an interesting paradox . . .*
> *Slow deep breathing is the fastest way*
> *from anxiety to calm.*

What You Say, Matters...
Naming Strategies to
Diminish Anxiety

Self-Affirmations

Who would have thought that self-affirmations could make a difference in easing anxiety given the tremendous amount of confusion and controversy about them? Affirmations are the positive self-statements (e.g., "I am beautiful", I am well liked and well respected", "I am wealthy") that have been consistently derided and satirized as ego driven, silly, and useless. Yet, psychologists Clayton Critcher and David Dunning believe affirmations act as a buffer or cushion against outside threats... what some might call the bitterness or harshness of life.

Affirmations can help you broaden your perspective, diminish defensiveness, mitigate and defuse criticism, stand up to what you perceive as an outside threat, and persevere when facing challenges. It's good news. If you use them already, science stands behind you. If you have never tried using them because it seemed so silly to do so, then know that they can help expand your emotional and cognitive flexibility so you can more successfully handle life challenges.

> *Affirmations help broaden your perspective*
> *so you can persevere through challenging times.*

Use Your Name to Talk to Yourself

What you say to yourself really matters. When you talk to yourself (and most people do), and you've done something you feel embarrassed about, do you say something like" "I'm such a dummy." or "Idiot, you can't do anything right"?

You might consider your self-talk mindless chatter, yet a growing body of research suggests that how you talk to yourself can make a big difference in how you handle your anxieties and fears and even the compassion you show yourself. More specifically, psychologist Ethan Kross and his colleagues discovered that how people talk to themselves has a significant impact on their success in life.

Here is his most interesting finding. If you talk to yourself with the pronoun 'I', you are more likely to perform less well when faced with stressful circumstances (e.g. competitions, public speaking or asserting yourself). Yet, if you address yourself by using your first name, then you increase your chances of effectively handling whatever you pursue. Instead of saying "I'm such an idiot." you would say something like "Jill, that was such an idiotic move."

By switching back and forth between how you address the self – whether it is first person (I, me) or third (using your first name) – you either move closer to or further away from your sense of self and emotional intensity. Especially when you experience strong feelings, using your name allows you to take a step back and get a little emotional distance from whatever is going on. Just that little bit of emotional detachment can have the effect of allowing you to advise and reason with yourself in the same wise manner that you would counsel a friend. Fair warning though – you don't want to use this self-talk approach to avoid your feelings. That can lead to a different set of problems.

Dr. Kross suggests this small shift in language from personal pronoun to first name can help minimize social anxiety. Overall, it leads to better performance, a more flexible thinking style and less rumination. This shift allows you to think through your own problems more wisely.

Just imagine what you can handle. Need to repair a conflict with a friend that you have been avoiding? Go into it saying *"Now, Abby, go ahead and call her. You've handled conflicts with friends before and had things turn out really well. Just stay calm. And if it doesn't work out, you'll be able to deal with it. You're smart, likeable and have lots of friends that love you. Just do your best. Abby, you got this girl."* Or maybe you'd want to use this approach for a first date, making a speech, asking for a raise, or . . .

> *Addressing yourself by using your first name*
> *can have the effect of allowing you to*
> *advise and reason with yourself*
> *in the same wise manner that you might counsel a friend.*

Feeling... Something

People often wonder why the experience of unpleasant (negative) emotions is so strong and why there are so many painful and unpleasant emotions. It's tied to evolution. Your survival is far more dependent on being able to be aware of and experience 'negative' emotions than experience pleasant ones. The truth is, that at the most basic level, it is these 'negative' emotions or emotional states that are involved in protecting us and in helping us survive in the world. So we absolutely need to be able to access and make use of them. Which makes them not "bad", nor "negative" feelings because they are so necessary for our survival. See them as just unpleasant or unsettling feelings as opposed to bad or negative ones.

Along with control over your behavior, you do have some control over *what* and *how* you think, so one way to manage your feelings is to consistently and intentionally practice thinking about what you feel.

That doesn't mean questioning and doubting what you feel. Instead, think of it as 'minding your mind'... as if you are watching a movie flash by on the screen of your mind. Developing this ability to notice what you are thinking and feeling can help you better choose how you would like to respond, no matter what situation you face.

However, you can't control *that* you feel or *what* you feel. Generally speaking, you are not in charge of the bodily sensations / feelings that you naturally experience in reaction to everyday life events. So you can't really 'control' your feelings – they are the surges of energy that let you know you're alive, allow you to experience a sense of aliveness and vitality, and they are elicited in response to your everyday life experiences, whether big or small. Rather than exerting control, you can, however, manage, modulate or modify your feeling experience once it is in your conscious awareness.

What I find fascinating is that bodily sensations help us know what we feel emotionally. It happens so quickly and seamlessly that most of us don't even realize this connection exists. It is my belief that *the bodily sensations that help us know what we're feeling is at the core of what makes it so hard to comfortably experience and handle feelings. It is the discomfort of these bodily sensations from which most people want to disconnect or distract.* It's not that you don't really want to feel what is coming up for you when you are anxious... instead it is the bodily sensation that lets you know what you are feeling that you don't want to experience. This is where the real problem lies with anxiety.

How – What – Where of Feelings

What follows is an exercise that will help you understand how feelings are linked with bodily sensations. In a moment this is what you can do is to find a comfortable position, take a few deep breaths – again, slowly take a deep breath in and then after a count of 4 or 6, exhale – and another deep breath in... and exhale... and one more deep breath in... and exhale.

Then, you'll close your eyes – and notice how, what and where you feel sad... angry... disappointed... content... deeply satisfied after successfully completing a long sought-after goal... joy... and the feeling of excited, happy anticipation. Simply notice how, what and where you experience the feelings above.

For example, sometimes when I feel sad, I get a light sensation that runs up and down my cheeks, and just underneath my eyes right before I tear up and cry. Perhaps you'll feel sadness or disappointment as a heaviness or dull ache centered near your heart. One past client of mine experienced anger as heat in the back of her neck and another felt anger as heat running across the top of both of her arms.

Stop reading and take a few moments to slowly walk yourself through each of the feelings. If you link the feeling mentioned to your specific memories of having that feeling, it may help bring your experience right to the surface. Go ahead and do it now.

Notice how, what and where you feel... sad... angry... disappointed...
content... deep satisfaction... joy...
and the feeling of excited, happy anticipation.

Use this page to write down *how* (e.g. sharp, pointed, dull, pulsing, intense), *what* and *where* you felt the bodily sensation(s) attached to each of the feelings below.

	How	What	Where
Sad			
Angry			
Disappointed			
Content			
Deeply satisfied			
Joy			
Excited anticipation			

Maybe you found that all your feelings were experienced in the same location in the same way or that it was hard to access any bodily sensations tied to any of your feelings. Perhaps you noticed each particular feeling had different bodily sensations linked to it. It's also possible that a few feelings seemed to be experienced the same way (like sadness and disappointment, for example) and the rest were more distinctly felt. Or that you experienced unpleasant feelings in your body as tighter, smaller or more constricting whereas the pleasant feelings left you feeling more relaxed, calmer, warmer, lighter or more expansive.

There is no right or wrong answer. How you experience a feeling is unique to you, yet it's important to understand the link between emotional feelings and bodily sensations. The 'How–What–Where' exercise is one way to help increase your awareness of this link between the two.

If you completed the *How-What-Where* exercise, then you have a growing awareness of how you experience some pleasant and unpleasant feelings within your body proper. You can use this approach to notice how you experience other pleasant and unpleasant feelings. And, if you haven't completed the exercise, now would be a great time to complete it. Information that relates to this exercise immediately follows on the next several pages.

Labeling Feelings

Why is accurately naming or labeling feelings so important? Dr. Matthew Lieberman, a UCLA psychologist, suggests that labeling feelings has the effect of shifting the emotional state to a thinking state. The shift can even be observed in the brain. Once feelings were labeled, there was less activity in the amygdala (the fight/flight center) and more activity in the right ventrolateral prefrontal cortex. This prefrontal area is in the thinking part of the brain.

Here is what this research finding means. Thinking about or reflecting on emotion is a great way to modulate and handle what you are feeling. So naming or labeling feelings can have multiple effects including those of calming or slowing you down, centering you, decreasing the experience of being flooded with feeling, decreasing impulsivity, and increasing a sense of control. And if you are really accurate, it can change your experience entirely, leaving you feeling more empowered, emotionally stronger, more confident and experiencing a calm inner peace.

> *Labeling feelings helps calm and center you,*
> *which increases your sense of control*
> *and helps you feel more empowered.*

Fear or Anxiety?

Though people often describe feeling fearful or frequently use the word 'fear' to describe what they are experiencing, I believe the word is both over and misused. Remember, the words you choose to use (e.g. fearful) can influence your decisions and actions. Stating you are fearful might lead you to withdraw rather than pursue your desired goal or goals.

Also remember *that fear is characterized by a clear and specific danger right now. In contrast, anxiety is characterized by that diffuse sense of apprehension about an aversive and formless danger in the future.* Similar to fear, anxiety* is known by bodily sensations such as a fast heartbeat, constriction in the chest, or a nervous feeling on the inside. Yet, it's important to determine: Is the danger or threat known and occurring right now, such that you are in immediate danger? Or is the danger or threat tied ambiguously to the future?

Choose which one you really feel by naming it more accurately. *Is it fear or anxiety? Are you fearful or anxious?* In most situations, it is much more likely that you will be experiencing anxiety rather than genuine fear. Use the more accurate word to describe what is happening. It can make a big difference. Borrowing a phrase from Dr. Daniel Siegel, "name it to tame it".

> *Are you facing*
> *a clear and present danger right now*
> *or a diffuse sense of apprehension*
> *about something in the future?*

Except, you can also consider whether it is...

Anxiety or Vulnerability?

Perhaps you would feel better if you identified your anxiety as vulnerability instead. Vulnerability, in this case, involves the awareness that you could get hurt. Feeling embarrassed or exposed is often linked with vulnerability and sometimes feeling vulnerable can leave you feeling "off center". Think about it. How many times have you felt anxious when you were really feeling vulnerable instead?

You can experiment with how that changes your experience right now. Think of situations where you felt anxious. Replace 'anxious' with 'vulnerable'? How does that change what you experience?

Do you have reasons to experience this diffuse apprehension known as anxiety? Absolutely yes! You are constantly faced with unexpected challenging, difficult, tragic or traumatic events that you cannot control, predict or prevent. And the world may be feeling a bit more uncertain and unsettling, especially in light of hostile, unpredictable and volatile intentional threats or acts of violence. The anxiety associated particularly with intentional terrorizing violence is quite obviously tied to concerns with physical survival and with the experience of being vulnerable.

Vulnerability involves the possibility of being hurt. When you consciously exert your choice to be vulnerable, think of it as the presence, openness, awareness and willingness to engage with other people, or in activities, where you might experience physical, mental or emotional pain. More simply, *vulnerability is an openness and willingness to learn and/or to feel hurt.*

For some, just being able to face and live everyday life feels vulnerable enough. For others, it may include many possible choices like public speaking, acting, drama, music, singing, entertainment, sports and displaying art as examples of "putting yourself out there", thus leaving you open to criticism, ridicule or some other manner of being hurt.

The truth is, at some level, you are always vulnerable – 24/7 – whether you are aware of it or not. So, there isn't a time when you aren't vulnerable - and this level of vulnerability is true for everyone. However, people who live in environments (e.g. war-torn countries, impoverished inner-cities, gang-controlled communities) and situations (e.g. domestic violence) where they constantly face dangerous or life-threatening experiences, live with a heightened consciousness and awareness of their vulnerability.

For those fortunate and privileged enough to live in safer environments, it is the ever-changing life situations or events (including natural disasters, unexpected tragedy, intentional violence) that calls into our awareness the experience of feeling vulnerable. If there is no danger or life threat present, and you are not being constantly reminded of it, then you tend not to think about nor feel particularly vulnerable. And, when trauma or tragedy happens - even at great geographical distance (floods, hurricanes, tornadoes, earthquakes, fires, oil spills, random workplace or school shootings, mining disasters, airplane crashes, unexpected and unanticipated sudden death or loss), then what changes is the degree to which we are aware we could suffer or be hurt – not necessarily the actual threat.

It's an important distinction. When tragic or traumatic circumstances arise, generally it is the degree to which you are aware that you could suffer or be hurt that has changed, as opposed to an actual threat or dangerous circumstance that you face. For instance, many Americans across the United States purchased survival related kits and supplies following the World Trade Center attack on September 11, 2001, despite the fact that residents of New York City experienced the greatest damage and were experiencing the greatest threat.

So, you feel more vulnerable mostly because you are more aware that you could be hurt. Of course, if you live in a dangerous or life-threatening situation, then you may naturally be more conscious of feeling vulnerable – otherwise, if you tend to live and work in generally safe and predictable environments, your awareness of feeling vulnerable tends to be in the background.

Legitimate concerns such as climate change, drought and water shortages, extreme weather patterns and an altered or damaged food supply can have the effect of keeping us aware of our vulnerability on a more constant basis. The constant barrage of threatening and damaging news from multiple media sources doesn't help. It amps up our experience of threat. If you hold the thoughts that you are so small and really, "just what can one person do" to effect change, then along with an experience of threat you may have feelings of helplessness and despair.

The goal, of course, is to turn your vulnerability into strength. First, remember that everyone else also feels some degree of vulnerability regardless of how conscious or honest they are about acknowledging this feeling. We will never fully escape this experience. The challenge is to maintain a low enough level of awareness about your vulnerability to choose to live fully, without it either emotionally paralyzing you or preventing you from taking action in life.

> *How often do you say you are anxious*
> *when you are really feeling vulnerable instead?*

Anxiety or Unexperienced and Unexpressed Feeling

Many times people state they feel fearful or anxious in place of what they are really feeling or thinking. As above, when they more accurately describe their thoughts and feelings, the experience of anxiety either significantly diminishes or it may go away entirely. It's quite likely you can benefit in a similar manner.

Parallel to the earlier strategies, this one also entails more accurately naming your experience. In this case, think of anxiety as *"unexperienced and unexpressed feelings"*. You'll understand anxiety from a new perspective from the following examples.

One afternoon, I was sitting with my good friend Glenda, and her best friend, Danielle. Glenda, a successful saleswoman in the highly competitive fashion industry, was talking about her challenges with ongoing anxiety and headache, and the many treatments she had pursued to experience consistent relief, though to little avail. She was anxious and in pain as we were talking and she wondered what I thought. I asked the first question that came to mind... how comfortable was she with sadness, crying and expressing anger. Her answer stunned me.

She was now 37 and hadn't cried since she was a teenager. And, no, she tended not to either acknowledge or express her anger. Given permission to ask more, I simply wondered what that was about. She answered with what most people say... she would look weak and vulnerable, she couldn't let her guard down, and she made references to the degree to which 'weaker' feelings were allowed in her household while growing up. They were not. And as she was talking, her lip was quivering to hold back tears.

We also talked about her reluctance to express her dismay and anger. With a little prompting she actually allowed herself to cry on and off for about twenty minutes. A few short minutes after that Glenda said her headache pain had lessened and she felt calmer and more peaceful inside. She recognized in those moments that she had not been allowing herself to be in touch with nor express much sadness, grief, anger and need... mostly because she didn't want to appear vulnerable nor weak.

DOWNLOAD FREE AND LISTEN TO

PODCAST #12
DOES CRYING REALLY MEAN YOU ARE EMOTIONALLY WEAK?

THE MINDSTREAM PODCAST
https://geo.itunes.apple.com/us/podcast/the-mindstream-podcast/id1034587865?mt=2

A quick conversation with Derrick, a model and actor, led to a similar "aha" moment for him and a change in how he experiences his own feelings. We were immersed in discussing movies and he started talking about how anxious he feels at certain times.

When I hear the word anxiety, I pay very close attention. It's like I'm on a mission to reorient and change the way people understand, experience and express anxiety. In Derrick's case, I only asked a couple quick questions. First, how – what – where did he experience the anxiety in his body. He touched and circled his hand all around his upper chest. Then I asked: "if I took all the words relating to anxiety away from you, what would you really be feeling?" Immediately he recognized it was really disappointment – a true "aha" moment. Days later when we talked, he described how he could readily attach his feeling of disappointment to a variety of experiences involving his father, that he had been sweeping under the carpet. He found that he could think about and make sense of those memories with much greater ease and was feeling less anxious and more empowered as a result.

Bob, a successful lawyer in his fifties, came to me initially describing fears that had started about two months before. He was now more concerned because they were persistent and unrelenting. One of his fears involved sleeping in the dark and the second was less clear; he just knew he felt afraid.

As we talked, he was able to shift his thinking from fear, to anxiety to his concerns about loss and loneliness. He didn't like to cry and hadn't really grieved the deaths of several family members and friends. When the lights were out at night, in the quiet of the dark, his thoughts would drift to thinking about those losses. In an effort to move away from that grief, particularly sadness, he would start to feel afraid and then insist the lights be left on so he could sleep.

He wasn't really afraid of the dark... it was really much more about the "darkness" of his sadness and grief. As he allowed himself to experience his genuine sadness, his concerns about sleeping in the dark went away. And, he recognized his loneliness had something to do with his decision to dismiss a long time employee at his firm. Remaining aware of the feelings he had been ignoring and pushing aside helped his anxiety subside.

I was several weeks into listening to Sally and Jane, two graduate psychology students enrolled in a group therapy course, each discuss their experience of anxiety when I finally wondered out loud whether it was really anxiety they were experiencing. My statement stopped them cold and piqued their curiosity.

These are the questions I posed for them. First, I asked if they were both interested in diminishing their experience of anxiety. The obvious answer, yes. Second, I asked each to identify an experience or memory when they felt anxious and to allow themselves to feel it, stating it wasn't necessary for me to know what they had identified. They did.

Next, I said: "If I took all the words away from you that were suggestive of anxiety, what would you really be feeling?" Sally said apprehensive and Jane said fearful. Both were suggestive of anxiety, so they couldn't use those two words. Then, Sally said sad; Jane followed with anger. I asked each one to go back to the memory they identified and for Sally to feel her sadness and Jane to feel her anger in their respective experiences. They did. Then, I asked if either one could experience the anxiety they had described earlier. The anxiety was not present for Sally, nor for Jane, and they both found this change in experience quite surprising.

I asked if the memories they had chosen involved other people. Once again, they both answered yes. I followed by asking if expressing the sadness and anger, respectively, would have been appropriate in each of the situations. Yet one more time it was a yes answer for both. Finally, I asked Sally if she had expressed her sadness and Jane if she had expressed her anger to the people involved in the situation. Both replied no. Knowing smiles fanned across their faces followed by sighs of relief and laughter.

Here's how to understand what took place. Sally and Jane were trying to keep true feelings that were present for each of them, out of their awareness... sadness for Sally, anger for Jane. In psychology, the mental effort to not think what you don't want to think is called thought suppression. I describe it as "trying not to know what you know". Except, thought suppression doesn't really work.

If I asked you to try not to think of a giraffe with stripes, your mind would conjure up the image of a giraffe with stripes. In an effort to not think what you don't want to think, you have to think it first, to then not think it. It doesn't make sense and it doesn't work.

If true feelings are not being experienced and not being expressed outwardly where they belong (especially when it is called for), they have to go somewhere. They get transmuted into anxiety and go inside instead of out. Once you accurately identify, feel and express your thoughts and feelings, then your "inside self" experience changes. It did change, by the way, for both Sally and Jane. Three weeks later they looked and sounded very different, and were far more confident and relaxed women!

> *If I took all the words away from you*
> *that were suggestive of anxiety, fear and worry,*
> *what would you really be feeling?*

You'll see the questions I posed for them are on the next page. Try it out for yourself. Use these questions as a guide to reset your anxiety. It's called the "Rosenberg Anxiety Reset™".

FREE RESOURCE

You can download and print a copy of this exercise.
Simply visit:

http://www.AnxietyFree.Space

Rosenberg Anxiety Reset™

1. Are you interested in diminishing or easing your experience of anxiety?

2. Identify an experience or memory when you felt anxious and allow yourself to feel it.

3. If I took all the words away from you that were suggestive of anxiety, fear or worry, what would you really be feeling? Apprehensive, fear, fearful, panicked and scared or any other similar words you can't use as part of your answer.

4. Go back to the experience or memory you identified and swap your anxiety or worry with this new feeling (from question 3) and stay with the experience for 5-10 seconds.

5. Can you feel or experience your previously described anxiety? (Most commonly, the answer is no.)

6. Did the memory/memories you chose involve other people?

7. Would expressing the feeling you identified have been appropriate in your situation?

8. Was this feeling expressed during that situation or a close time after the situation?

Anxiety as a Cover for Unpleasant Feelings

Many people describe "feeling anxious" or "having anxiety", when, in fact, the anxiety is really other feelings that people have turned inward on themselves rather than express them outwardly to others. We saw that in the example above, particularly with Sally and Jane where anxiety was experienced in place of anger and sadness.

So anxiety itself, oddly, is used as a means (conscious or not) to distract or disconnect from something that is harder to bear, feel or know. Feeling anxious because you don't want to feel angry or sad? The feeling has to go somewhere so it becomes anxiety. It's all about disconnecting and distracting from those same unpleasant feelings. Another way, then, to think about anxiety is that it is either a cover over or a distracter from a variety of unpleasant feelings.

Think of worry / anxiety as a cover – much like an umbrella protecting something underneath. To see what I mean, put your left hand with a closed fist directly in front of you. That closed left fist represents unpleasant feelings. With the left hand remaining in position, put your right hand, curved like an umbrella, a few inches directly above your left hand. The right hand is what you call anxiety and is a cover for one or more of your unpleasant feelings. My goal is to take the cover away (your right hand) so you can be aware of what you are really feeling. Once you are aware and in touch with the real feeling, the anxiety dissipates or diminishes greatly and then it is a matter of "riding the wave(s)" of unpleasant feelings to make your way through them.

For instance, if I'm really angry and disappointed about something that my friend Chelsea did – perhaps something like sharing information with others that I asked Chelsea not to share – and that I'm the type of person who hates having conflicts with others ... and I also have a hard time saying what I really mean... then I'm likely to not address the issue with Chelsea... preferring instead to shut out or let my feelings of anger and disappointment pass... and of course, acting like nothing is wrong between Chelsea and me.

Haven't you ever done something similar?

If I actually behaved just as I described above, then I start feeling uncomfortable or anxious inside – especially because I am trying to suppress my reactions (or "not know what I know") ... sort of trying to hide my own truth or my own experience of reality from myself... **and** ... in this example, I am also hiding that truth from Chelsea.

To soften what I'm experiencing, so I can continue to be friends with Chelsea and not rock the boat – I end up changing my experience of anger and disappointment into feelings of anxiety. What would have been initially directed outward towards Chelsea so it could be discussed between us is now directed inward against me.

It's almost like anxiety is the socially acceptable experience to have – versus the real feelings that are harder to bear that could potentially hurt someone else. It's messy and uncomfortable. And what the anxiety umbrella is covering is the experience of unpleasant feelings like sadness, anger, disappointment or frustration.

The key is to become aware of the true feelings you might be experiencing in a situation, no longer use your anxiety as a cover or distracter, experience, and then, with discretion, express your real feeling(s) if it is appropriate to do in the given situation.

> *Do you tend to worry, be anxious or preoccupied?*
> *What feelings do your anxiety and worry cover up?*

Anxiety as Doubt and Disbelief in Being Capable and Resourceful

Anxiety acts like radar for me. If you tend to experience a lot of anxiety, it's a signal that you may have a hard time managing unpleasant feelings, yet your experience of feeling capable in the world emerges out of your ability to handle them. If you don't let yourself experience unpleasant feelings or you don't do it well, then generally speaking, you won't feel fully capable.

Nor will you feel resourceful. Resourcefulness involves feeling vulnerable and vulnerability enables you to acknowledge your needs and limitations, reach out to others and ask for help.

Nor will you assert yourself by speaking up, saying what you want to say when you want to talk and with whom you want to talk.

It makes anxiety seem almost circular. Finding it hard to handle unpleasant feelings leads to feeling less capable and resourceful, and without feeling capable and resourceful, you feel anxious! So when you say you're anxious, what you are actually conveying is that you don't believe you can handle the anticipated feeling outcome of whatever you are facing.

If you feel capable – meaning you can handle unpleasant feelings – then there are fewer reasons to feel anxious because you already know you can handle the feeling result of things not working out the way you want.   One of the major resolutions of anxiety, then, is to be able to comfortably experience and express unpleasant feelings.

You can think of anxiety, then, as doubt and disbelief in your capacity to be capable and resourceful.

> *Anxiety is doubt and disbelief*
> *in your capacity to be capable and resourceful.*

Anxiety and
Questions and Statements

Anxiety is a future-oriented feeling whereas most other feelings we experience are tied to the past. When people are worried and anxious, they are either anticipating a future event will somehow turn negative or they simply anticipate only negative events. But it doesn't end there.

Anxiety and "What If" Questions

My friend and colleague, Brendon Burchard, author of *The Manifesto*, likes to say that people feel anxious because they ask "what if" questions followed by some negative statement. If asking those "what if" questions is something that you do, here are a few more strategies that can make a huge difference for you.

Your brain will try to answer whatever question or problem you pose – so if you ask questions that elicit negative thoughts, well, your brain will be all too eager to oblige and come up with thoughts, feelings and memories that fit your question.

If you pose "what if" questions that are usually followed by a negative statement, now match that negative statement with a positive one. Better yet, ask positively oriented questions and make positive statements, then your brain will oblige just as willingly in that direction.

> *Match your negative statement with a positive one.*

You can ask your "what if" question and then follow it directly with a positive statement ... Like "what if this event turned out so much better than I expected?" "what if I met someone here that I really connected with?" "what if something really good happened today that went beyond my wildest expectations?"

> Follow your "what if" with a positive statement.

Change your "what if" questions to "what is" statements and then look at the evidence around you to decrease your anxiety. One person used this approach to decrease her fear of flying. Her worry was about a plane crash... "what if the plane goes down?" While on the plane and into her worry, she was guided to look around and describe to herself what she noticed.

So she could say: *"what is happening right now* is that we're in flight and it's calm, people are reading and sleeping, the weather is good, my seat partners are interesting" – and on and on.

> Change your "what if" questions to "what is?" statements.
> Look at the evidence at hand to diminish your worry and anxiety.

Anxiety and the
"Can I, Will I, Am I" Questions

There are a number of other questions people ask themselves that maintain feelings of anxiety – questions that lead to and foster doubt. These are the *"Can I?" "Will I?" "Am I" questions.* "Will I be able to deliver a good presentation?" "Will I do a good job?" "Will they like me?" "Can I really pull this off?" "Can I achieve what I want to achieve?" "Am I okay?" "Am I going to be able to complete this project?"

These type of questions simply increase doubt and doubt increases the experience of worry and anxiety. Doubt leads to a loss of power and control. Doubt leads to believing you are less capable. Doubt leads to a lack of a sense of resourcefulness. Doubt leads to less confidence.

Remember, whatever you ask your brain, your brain will do its best to answer for you. So, *the strategy* for addressing these anxiety-maintaining questions *is to change your question into statements. Make declarative sentences and switch the order of your words...*

> 'Can I' becomes 'I can'
>
> 'Will I' becomes 'I will'
>
> 'Am I' becomes 'I am'

For instance, rather than asking "will I do a good job?", turn that question into a statement instead and say to yourself: "I will do a good job." And if you ask "how will I" then change that question into a statement of "I will find a way to . . .".

You can also say to yourself: "I am capable and resourceful." It may seem basic to say those words, yet making that switch from a question that raises doubt into a statement that conveys being grounded and confident really does make a difference in how you experience yourself internally. Countless individuals have greatly benefited from consistent practice of this one phrase.

Just try it for a few seconds right now. And with each new or difficult situation you encounter, keep reminding yourself of your ability to be capable and resourceful. Keep rehearsing this phrase over and over in your mind. Remember, you are shooting for 66-90 days of mental rehearsal.

Asking "Can I? Will I? Am I?" questions maintains anxiety.

Say instead: "I can... I will... I am..."

Or

Say: "I am capable and resourceful"

to diminish your doubt and increase your confidence.

Anxiety and Decisions

Choose Growth over Fear, Anxiety or Worry

An element that can make a big difference in your capacity to live a life you love – one that is more free of worry – is tied to how well you understand growth and protection.

Dr. Bruce Lipton, a well-known cell biologist, suggests that we are all programmed for the processes of growth and protection. For example, he described how cells exhibit a growth response when they gravitate to nutrients and a protective response when they retreat from toxins. He suggests we humans (who happen to be multicellular organisms) behave similarly.

However, these processes cannot operate at their highest level simultaneously. Lipton notes that growth is a process that both expends and produces energy; thus, "a sustained protection response inhibits the creation of life-sustaining energy" (p.116). The longer you stay in a protection mode (i.e., anxious or worried) the more you deplete your energy reserves, which in turn, can compromise your growth.

Consequently, you can't really be fully engaged in activities of protection and growth at the same time. That's like trying to go in two opposite directions simultaneously. It's rather challenging to attempt to do both concurrently and still function in an optimal manner.

Just as cells in a laboratory dish retreat from toxins, as humans we (generally) do our best to retreat from toxic situations (danger, aggression, threat, chaos, confusion). However, energy depleting worry and anxiety may keep weaving you in and out of the toxicity.

You tend to engage in life-sustaining activities when you feel safe. With safety, you may seek opportunities to connect with others, play, attach and bond closely with them or provide nurturance, support, encouragement, love, and kindness.

If you don't have to expend physical or emotional energy on protecting yourself, then you can gravitate to experiences that involve growth, namely, connecting with others and creativity. When you feel safe, you are more likely to explore, investigate, exhibit curiosity and interest, search for and pursue experiences that elicit a sense of purpose and meaning.

What you choose to believe also has a huge impact on your overall health and well-being.

Think of it this way: living in fear leads to compromised health and a protective response from your body; living from a place of love, kindness, compassion and gratitude leads to growth.

These positive qualities promote growth. And, if you consistently inhibit your growth process, you significantly compromise your vitality. It's important, then, to pursue experiences that are fulfilling and bring you joy. Choose growth.

> *Anxiety, fear and worry*
> *deplete the energy reserves you need for growth.*
> *Choose growth.*

Choose Easy over Difficult, Hard or Struggle

Remember, there is a tendency for anxious and worried people to ask "what if" questions followed by negative statements, and that the net effect of these questions and statements is that it increases anxiety. Remember, too, that your brain will try to answer whatever question or problem you pose – so if you ask questions that elicit negative thoughts, then your brain will come up with thoughts, feelings and memories that fit your question.

Similarly, there is a tendency to expect that life will be difficult and painful and that goals and dreams take a long time to come to fruition. Notice how tempted you are to make things difficult, hard or a struggle. Really, what if it were easy?

So, as you practice asking more positively oriented questions and statements, also practice anticipating that things can happen in your life that come with ease, grace, speed and joy. It's in keeping with the theme of this book... helping you change both what and how you think so you can lead a freer, fuller and more expressed life.

> *Choose and anticipate that*
> *your life will be one of ease, grace and joy.*

Schedule Your Worry

Consider scheduling your worry. Designate a certain amount of time to worry each day, every couple days, once a week or every couple weeks as a way to rein in your unbridled worries. If you are worrying outside your scheduled time, simply note your worry and remind yourself that you are only allowed to take up that concern at the specific time(s) you have scheduled. Then, redirect your thinking to the task at hand. Notice how successful you become at redirecting your thinking to the proper task at hand.

Consequences and Loss

An experience of anxiety may also result if there is a decision to be made and you feel pulled in two directions with choices that feel pretty equal to you. Besides writing out the traditional "pro-and-con" list that people often recommend in this situation, here are two other suggestions.

First, set aside roughly twenty minutes to sit quietly and just focus on deep breathing and quieting your mind. When you feel fully relaxed, take each available choice for your situation and run through your mind how you see it playing out, from beginning to end. Pay special attention to the feelings each choice elicits, whether pleasant or unpleasant. Also consider the consequences in the short-term (over the next few weeks or months) and the long-term (what the effects of your choice may be say 3, 5, or 10 years from now).

Second, decisions, by their very nature, imply loss. One thing gets chosen and one or more do not. Sometimes you experience anxiety over having to face an anticipated loss. Loss is tied to sadness, anger and disappointment. Sometimes you avoid decisions so you won't have to deal with those three feelings. Instead, you just feel anxious.

Returning to that relaxed state, take some time to absorb what your experience of loss may be if you were to make one choice over the other.

> *With decisions you need to make...*
> *take time to think about the short- and long-term consequences*
> *and the losses that may accompany your decision.*

Anxiety and Taking Action

Consider this thought...

> *That which you worry about or are preoccupied with,*
> *you either are already experiencing*
> *or you are in the process of creating.*

I often talk with people who are disappointed because they don't have more friends, yet they are afraid to exert the effort it takes to develop them. As a result, they feel really disappointed with the way their life is going. And, they end up doing a lot of things alone, when they could actually be calling people they know to get together. But they don't make those calls because they are afraid of being disappointed. So the very experience they worry about feeling (in this case, feeling disappointed), they had already been experiencing (disappointed because they didn't have more friends).

Your worry is an interesting paradox. Usually the very events and situations you are afraid of experiencing, you already have some success at managing. Realizing this, it might make it easier to go after your goals and dreams. Taking action is the resolution. You develop the capacity to handle unpleasant feelings and begin to build confidence simultaneously.

> *Taking action is one resolution to worry.*
> *It helps you handle unpleasant feelings*
> *and builds confidence simultaneously.*

Worry can also involve a lack of belief and trust in your capacity to handle tasks and logistics. It's tied to the lack of belief in your own capability and resourcefulness. Research about people who worry suggests that *worriers tend to repeat the same worry over and over in their mind rather than take their worries to a logical conclusion or end point* (e.g., "what's the worst that could happen"). Likewise, they rarely consider what they will need or what they can do once they reach that end point.

Let's say that you are worried about getting to an appointment on time that is twenty-five minutes from your home. As an example of your worry, you may be just repeating a couple thoughts over and over that sound like: "Uh oh – what'll happen if I don't get there on time. I'm worried about getting there since I don't know what the traffic will be like. What if I hit traffic? I'm afraid of not getting there on time? What if I have car trouble? What if something happens along the way?"... and on and on and on.

Sound familiar? Just change the script to fit your specific worries.

Let's delve into the concern that you'll hit traffic on the way to that important appointment. So, you *ask yourself either "what's the worst that could happen" or "what if it did, then what?"* Your answer will lead you to identify the logistical or emotional resources you'll need to capably handle the situation.

A super important reminder for you here – when you come up with your answer, actually see yourself completing that task – **first, visualize** yourself actually doing what your answer says, and if it requires it, **then physically do what your answer suggests**.

Back to the example.

So, what if you hit traffic?

> *Well, you might need to leave earlier than you initially planned.*

What if you left early and there's an accident on the road?

Then you need to figure out an alternate route.

What if you're not familiar with the area?

Then you need to take some time and figure out alternate routes to travel before you go.

Just keep asking and answering till your worry about that given situation has been taken to its logical end. Along the way, you will have identified all the information you'll need (which by itself often reduces worry and anxiety), you will be completing different tasks or you'll develop new skills to make sure you have the necessary resources to handle the situation.

In addition to not walking worries out to their logical conclusion or end point, remember, *you may also worry because you don't see yourself as having the emotional resources to cope with the anticipated negative event you worry about, and also in an effort to have mastery over feeling(s) that have not yet occurred.*

As you face these events and situations, remember that many times reducing your anxiety doesn't involve getting new information or completing tasks... instead it involves the emotions you'll feel if something doesn't go the way you wanted or expected. What if you get frustrated? Or angry? Or disappointed? In this case, it's important to believe you have the available emotional resources to handle the situation if that happens.

So what are the emotional resources? The capacity to handle unpleasant feelings... feelings such as sadness, anger, disappointment and frustration. Start to believe that you are capable and have the resourcefulness to handle whatever challenges you'll face. Remember, worry, anxiety and preoccupation are often distracters from unpleasant feelings. Focus on the real feelings underneath and your anxiety can dissipate rather quickly.

Resourcefulness Reset™

Here's what you can do to diminish your worry anxiety. First, grab your pen, paper or computer. With each worry question you have, ask yourself either *what's the worst thing that would happen if your worry situation came to pass*, and ask yourself... *"what if it did, then what?"*

I want you to write out every answer you have to those two questions. Make sure you also write down the feelings you might face if that event or situation occurred. Keep writing till you reach a sense of completeness on the question. Then, read your initial worry concern and, one by one, read each of your responses to your worry. Visualize each response... see yourself effectively handle the situation whether it involves your feelings or something to be said or done. Once you make your way through the entire list, take a moment to check in and see if the intensity of your worry diminished.

> *Believe and trust in your own resourcefulness...*
> *your ability to effectively handle tasks, logistics*
> *and unpleasant feelings.*

DOWNLOAD FREE AND LISTEN TO

PODCAST #9
RELIEVE YOUR ANXIETY AND WORRY WITH THE
"RESOURCEFULNESS RESET™"

THE MINDSTREAM PODCAST
https://geo.itunes.apple.com/us/podcast/the-mindstream-podcast/id1034587865?mt=2

Anxiety and Congruence

Here's one other possibility for understanding and responding to your anxious feelings. *Worry or anxiety may be your bodily response to incongruence or your bodily response to disconnecting, distracting or suppressing what you know to be true for you.*

Remember the example I used about feeling angry with Chelsea but I didn't talk to her about the incident and my anger? This was an example of suppressing feelings. Instead, because I didn't talk to her, I ended up feeling anxious or uncomfortable inside because I was trying to hide the truth of my experience from me and from her.

Think about congruence as a person's actions matching their words, and their words and actions matching their thoughts and feelings. So, incongruence is when there is a mismatch among any of these elements. Your thoughts could be different from your feelings, your words could be different from your thoughts and feelings, your actions could be different from your words, and your actions could be different from your beliefs or your values. What happens, then, is that *a person feels anxious because he or she moves away from the truth of his or her experience* – and is somehow living inconsistent with that truth.

The fix to the incongruence is to live as fully present as you can – so all aspects of your experience match up... your actions match your words, your words and actions match your thoughts and feelings, and your thoughts, feelings, words and actions match your beliefs and values. When you do this, there won't be anxiety... instead there will be confidence, calm inner peace and a feeling of being comfortable in your own skin.

Are you living a congruent and fully present life?

How to Handle
Your Worry about
What Others Think of You

One of the most common and frequent concerns people express is their worry about what others think about them. If this is something you struggle with as well, just know you are in good company. People get very preoccupied or worried about what others are thinking about them, sometimes to such a degree that they either cancel or decline social events and invitations.

Worries may sound like: "they'll think that I'm too fat" (or too ugly, not attractive or smart enough) or "I'm gonna sound stupid", "they hate what I'm wearing", "they're just going to laugh at me"... and on, and on, and on. Do you do this too?

Let's break down these concerns. First, when you worry about what others may be thinking, it puts your center of attention and emotional or personal power outside yourself and into other people. You lose sight of what is important to you including what you think, feel, sense or need; how you experience other people; and how you experience the world.

Imagine standing in the center of a circle of people and looking through your own eyes at all the people around you. This is your position of personal power. Imagine next that a number of people were standing around that circle looking in at you – and you were trying to live in the world looking through their eyes before you could look through your own. In this second situation you are off balance, the energy is coming from outside the circle and you lose your sense of personal power. This is what it feels like when you are trying to live your life through others' eyes.

Worry about how you are perceived by others can become a preoccupation that simply dominates your thinking. Yet, this focus on what other people might be thinking about you (actually, what *you think* they are thinking about you) is really *just a distracter from feeling vulnerable*. Oddly enough, the truth is that most people worry about what you worry about... they worry about what you might be thinking about them!

> *Are you preoccupied with what others think of you?*
>
> *What feelings are you distracting yourself from?*

Thinking about what (you think) others think about you puts you in a real conundrum. When you are young, you need the observations, feedback and connection with others to help your brain develop... and the nature of your connections with others makes a difference in how your brain structures develop and how effectively your brain processes work. As you age, the feedback is useful, but if you rely too heavily on others' views of you, you never develop enough trust, confidence and ease expressing yourself.

Constructive feedback is valuable throughout your life, yet think of the percentage you rely on it to guide you, as subject to change... in the early part of your life, you need a much higher percentage or proportion of feedback from others to develop your brain and to develop your sense of self. It comes first from your parents or caregivers, then from teachers, coaches or other mentors. As you move into later childhood and adolescence, parents and other authority figures may take a bit of a back seat; instead you rely on peer feedback (whether it is genuinely useful or comes at the expense of bullying) to influence how you see yourself.

To some degree, thinking about what others think of you can be valuable – the feedback and guidance provided to you by others can help you change and grow. As you age and move into and through adulthood, the key is to rely on such feedback a much smaller percentage of time. The challenge is that grown men and women often continue to rely heavily on what they presume other people think about them to guide how they think, feel, make decisions and act. Yet you may currently feel like you get lost and overwhelmed by your worry about what others think about you.

In the ideal then, as you age, the amount of influence from others diminishes and you feel more capable of making decisions for yourself, while also making use of wise counsel to help you think through or guide some of your decision-making.

Think of it this way. From roughly birth to your middle twenties (25-27 years), you use feedback from others to help **define** yourself. After your middle twenties, you would use others' feedback to help **refine** yourself.

> *Feedback and wise counsel remain important throughout life.*
> *In your youth it is to help **define** you.*
> *As you age, it is to help **refine** you.*

Neuroscience offers some explanation as to why we pay so much attention to what others think about us. Paying attention to others is hard-wired into us. Whether aware of it or not, we are <u>always</u> assessing others and the environment for safety, danger and life threat.

We constantly monitor what is happening around us to determine how safe we are, how safe we perceive the people around us or how safe the environment is, so it makes sense that you could easily move into more significant worry about what others think of you. Showing concern with how you are viewed or even that you are being viewed is and can be helpful, enabling you to protect yourself in situations of threat or danger.

However, when worrying about how others see you becomes extreme or becomes the dominant focus of your life, it can constrict your life and become quite painful and even debilitating. I believe this type of worry is the cause of a lot of social anxiety, and if you could lessen your worry about how others view you, or how you think others view you, then you can enjoy your life a whole lot more.

If you: think others are thinking about you; tend to be overly concerned with what others think of you (or more accurately *what you think others think of you*); are afraid of making mistakes in front of others; are afraid of being ridiculed or laughed at or thought stupid; are afraid to take risks; are shy; hate public speaking; can't stand using the phone; or are afraid of social gatherings, then this information can be really helpful to you.

Let's start by having you answer a few questions.

First, *what percent of the time are people thinking about you as you go about your daily life?*

Now, if you're like most people, what you actually answered is a different question: *"What percent of the time* do you think *people are thinking about you?"* Just because you think they are thinking about you doesn't mean they are.

So now go ahead and answer that question: *What percent of the time* do you think *people are thinking about you?*

Second, *what percent of the time do you think people are actually* thinking the exact same thought *you think they are thinking about you?*

Third, *when you are busy worrying about or thinking about what you think other people are thinking about you, what are you missing?*

You miss:

a. being aware of your own experience – what you think, feel, sense or need
b. what you think about others
c. what you think about the world around you

You lose sight of your own experience. You take yourself out of the present moment and out of your own experience, which makes it so you can't know what you think or experience about yourself, or for yourself. You don't really know what is going on inside of you.

If you are so worried about what you think others may be thinking of you then you can't notice what you think about others and your experience of or with them. And, you can't notice what your experience is of the world around you.

That type of thinking... worrying about (what you think) others are thinking about you, I call: *"thinking from the outside in".*

You can't really know what other people are thinking... you can only guess. You'll know if you ask – and if you ask, you'll find out the other person's focus was rarely, if ever, on you.

The pattern of "thinking from the outside in" is mostly just a cover for feeling vulnerable.

Rather than feel vulnerable, embarrassed or exposed, *you try to take control of your vulnerable feelings by "thinking" instead* – yet you go one step further by assuming that others are thinking it about you instead of you thinking whatever you were thinking.

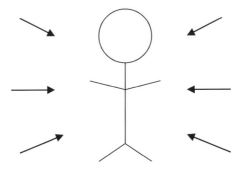

Figure 1: Thinking From the Outside-In

For example, let's say you put on a couple pounds. You go walking at the mall and all you do is worry that all the people that see or know you notice your couple pound weight gain and you believe all of them are thinking that you are fat. It's your thought about your own weight gain, yet in your mind, you make the assumption that anyone that sees you or knows you thinks you are fat.

> *The pattern of "thinking from the outside in"*
> *is mostly just a cover for feeling vulnerable.*

So what can you do about this concern about being judged?

Below is a nine-step strategy for diminishing your worry about what others think of you. If you find it hard to get out and socialize with others, re-working your thoughts in this manner can make it much easier for you to connect with others.

The Projection Correction™:
Nine Steps to Reclaim Your Personal Power

1. Keep my caring in mind, then look at the bold challenge to this worry:

    What makes you think you are *so special* that others are spending so much time thinking about you anyway? (Remember, most people are doing the same thing you are doing... they are worrying about what you are thinking about them rather than thinking about you.) Now, I know the last thing you may be thinking is that you are special, however this particular worry about what others may be thinking about you has the focus centered on you. This focus needs to change, especially since it is usually incorrect.

2. The type of thinking you are engaging in is often a *projection*...

    You are taking how you experience yourself or what you are thinking about yourself, and you are putting it onto other people and then assuming that they are thinking it about you. Remember the example of walking in the mall – you knew that you had put on a couple pounds yet you have everyone you see thinking you put on weight, or are fat, or...

3. You have to notice this "outside-in" thinking pattern.

    Notice that you are busy worrying or thinking about (what you think) other people are thinking about you. Notice that you may be projecting your thoughts or experience of yourself and assuming they are thinking *your thoughts* about you.

4.   Once you are aware of your "outside-in" thinking pattern, you need to

Actively shift your style of thinking and <u>decide</u> to *"think from the inside out"*.

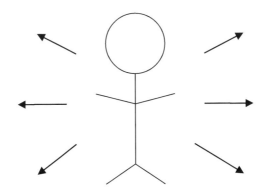

Figure 2 "Thinking from the inside out"

5.   Once you realize you are lost in this pattern of worry or thinking, stop:

Ask yourself if it is really likely that others are thinking about you, and if they are likely to be thinking the exact thought you think they are thinking about you.

6.   As you stay aware of your "outside-in" thinking or worry pattern...

Realize that thinking in this manner is a distraction from thoughts or feelings that are unpleasant and uncomfortable for you – and that these unpleasant thoughts or feelings may have nothing to do with the specific thoughts you were worried about. Here, ask yourself *"what uncomfortable or unpleasant thoughts or feelings am I trying to keep out of my awareness?"*

7.   "Outside-in" thinking tends to be also be a distraction from feeling vulnerable, so

Ask yourself "what am I feeling vulnerable about?"

8.   Remind yourself (again) that

What you think others are thinking about you is more likely what you are instead thinking about yourself. Reminding yourself that you are projecting your thoughts and experience onto others can help you deepen your resolve to live your life from the "inside-out"... it's the only way you can develop high confidence and self-esteem.

9.   Remember,

When you are lost in thinking about what you think others are thinking about you, you have stepped out of experiencing the present moment and you have stepped outside of your own experience. Your center of power is now outside of you and located in other people. You need to redirect yourself back into both your own experience and the present moment, and you can best do this by asking yourself: *"What do I need, think, feel or perceive right now?"* When you do that, you will regain your sense of power and a greater sense of control.

DOWNLOAD FREE AND LISTEN TO

PODCAST #3:
HOW TO STOP WORRYING ABOUT WHAT OTHERS THINK OF YOU

THE MINDSTREAM PODCAST
https://geo.itunes.apple.com/us/podcast/the-mindstream-podcast/id1034587865?mt=2

Putting It All Together

I started consulting with Bobby, a 20 year old man who is really interested, actually devoted, to his goal of getting into a great university, getting an athletic scholarship and then eventually transitioning into playing on a professional sports team. However, he had been struggling with anxiety, to such a significant degree that he was shaking all the time and he was also experiencing some panic symptoms. He described how he doubts and questions himself, and when it comes to achieving his sports dream, he said he is not playing up to his own capabilities on his current intramural team.

As we talked, the first thing I observed was his breathing. It was very shallow and high up in his chest. That is where my attention went first, and I had him take 15 consecutive deep slow breaths all the way down to the base of his diaphragm with a 6 count inhale and 4 count hold and then a 6 count exhale. His response? He stopped shaking and felt calmer right away. I asked him to keep practicing this type of breathing throughout our conversation.

It's well known that fast, shallow breathing can elicit most of the other panic symptoms, so getting him to slow down was the first order of business. Remember the paradox? Slow deep breathing is the fastest way to calm.

Given the level of his doubt and questioning, I explored how he handles unpleasant feelings. In his case, I was most curious about disappointment, sadness and vulnerability. Initially he said he handled them well, including talking with family members and friends about when he felt that way, yet as our conversation proceeded he acknowledged that maybe he wasn't so good about letting himself experience feeling vulnerable and disappointed. He said he actually hadn't experienced many disappointments throughout his life, so I suggested that maybe this time in his life was designed to help him face and tolerate disappointments, something psychologists call "frustration tolerance". If he could develop greater frustration tolerance, he could feel more capable and effective throughout adulthood.

I talked with him about how much he allowed himself to be caught up in his doubts and suggested that perhaps these doubts were his way of fending off his own feelings of sadness or disappointment if things didn't work out the way he wanted – especially given how highly invested he is in his desired outcomes.

My next efforts were focused on helping him understand he was more capable and resourceful than he saw himself. He had recently ended a three-year relationship (so he could handle sadness and disappointment); he had experienced other relationship losses (more sadness); he had had multiple coaching sessions to improve his skills to the highest level possible (disappointment and frustration), and he had handled countless other experiences too numerable to mention that involved experiencing unpleasant feelings. Would he consider then, that he was more capable of handling disappointment and similar unpleasant feelings as it related to his goals and dreams, if they were to occur in the future... especially given that he already knew how to handle them. He said yes.

Worrying about how he was seen by others was also a big challenge. To address this concern, I first reminded him that this worry was a distraction from feeling vulnerable. He needed to make the shift from "thinking from the outside in" to thinking from the inside out".

Then I asked the name of his favorite sports player (let's say Stan) and if he spent any time watching Stan on TV or on any available videos. He said yes, though the time viewing was limited. I asked him to find more video footage, to watch it and while he was watching it, I wanted him to see himself in Stan's shoes on the field. Then he was to imagine he was the one either defending or scoring as his sports idol. And, before he was to get on the field to play with his team again, he was to imagine that he was Stan putting on his sports gear and stepping onto the field. While on the field, he was to stay focused on playing as Stan played, as opposed to timidity or holding back.

At the end of our conversation I asked him to get more attached to his dream. What did he really want? What was going to keep him from getting there? What obstacles would he let stand in his way? He had already ended a relationship and moved to a different area in order to be more focused; was he really going to let his doubts and anxiety and reluctance to play full out get the best of him?

All of those suggestions were part of our first conversation. Bobby's response one week later was to say that he had already noticed big changes.

These strategies can open new possibilities for you. You have several different ones to consider. As you consider them, remember to seek appropriate counsel. Perhaps you'll choose one and get started. If you do, track your progress and observations by journaling. Then take action with another. Reflect on what you are noticing about your thoughts and feelings. Adjust. Keep going... remember you are going for 66-90 days straight. Persist. And then revel in the fact that you are designing your life and have what it takes to go after your dreams.

Be In Touch

Use several of these strategies and let me know how they work for you. You can hear more about handling anxiety and other challenges on The MindStream Podcast.

FREE RESOURCES
Remember to download and print copies of the exercises in this book. Simply visit:

http://www.AnxietyFree.Space

LISTEN AND SUBSCRIBE TO
THE MINDSTREAM PODCAST
https://geo.itunes.apple.com/us/podcast/the-mindstream-podcast/id1034587865?mt=2

If you love what you've read and what you've heard, please leave a review on Amazon and iTunes.

Visit my website: www.DrJoanRosenberg.com

And of course, follow me on social media.

- Twitter: @DrJoanRosenberg
- LinkedIn: DrJoanRosenberg
- Facebook Fan Page:

   https://www.facebook.com/pages/Dr-Joan-Rosenberg/613560995437748?ref=hl

References

Critcher, C. R., Dunning, D., & Armor, D. A. (2010). When self-affirmations reduce defensiveness: Timing is key. *Personality and Social Psychology Bulletin, 36*(7), 947-959.

Kross, E., Bruehlmann, E., Park, J., Burson, A., Dougherty, A., Shablack, H., Bremner, R., Moser, J., & Ayduk, O. (2014). Self talk as a regulatory mechanism: How you do it matters. *Journal of Personality and Social Psychology, 106*(2), 304–324.

Lieberman, M. D. Inagaki, T. K., Tabibnia, G., & Crockett, M. J. (2011). Subjective responses to emotional stimuli during labeling, reappraisal, and distraction. *Emotion, 3,* 468-480.

Lipton, B. (2008). *The biology of belief: Unleashing the power of consciousness, matter and miracles.* Hay House: Carlsbad, CA.

About The Author

 Joan I. Rosenberg, Ph.D., is an acclaimed global speaker, trainer, consultant, media host and master clinician. A cutting-edge psychologist who is known as an innovative thinker, trainer and speaker she has been recognized for her influence as a thought leader through her membership in the Association of Transformational Leaders (a regional offshoot of Jack Canfield's Transformational Leadership Council).

A California-licensed psychologist, Dr. Rosenberg speaks on how to build confidence, high self-esteem, core emotional strength and resilience; emotional, conversational and relationship mastery; neuroscience and psychotherapy; clinical supervision; and suicide prevention. She has shared stages with bestselling authors and personal development trainers (Brendon Burchard, John Assaraf, Mary Morrissey, Bo Eason, Daniel Siegel, JJ Virgin, John Gray, Michael Gelb, Norm Shealy, Barbara DeAngelis, and others).

Dr. Rosenberg has been featured in the critically acclaimed documentaries *"I Am"* directed by Tom Shadyac, *"The Hidden Epidemic"* directed by Bill Brown and featuring Dr. Daniel Amen and *"Pursuing Happiness"* with director, Adam Shell. She's been seen on CNN's *American Morning*, the OWN network and PBS, as well as appearances and radio interviews in all of the major metropolitan media markets. She is the creator and host of **The MindStream Podcast** on iTunes. She is the co-author of *Mean Girls, Meaner Women* as well as numerous professional articles for professional and trade journals.

Dr. Rosenberg maintains an independent consulting and coaching practice in Los Angeles, CA. A full-time professor at Pepperdine

University, she provides clinical supervision and teaches in the doctoral program in psychology at the Graduate School of Education and Psychology at Pepperdine University in Los Angeles, CA. As a United States Air Force veteran, she served as a psychologist in the Air Force as well as a staff psychologist at the University of California, Los Angeles. She also taught in graduate psychology programs at the University of Southern California and Phillips Graduate Institute in southern California and Wright State University in Dayton, OH. Dr. Rosenberg lives in Los Angeles, CA.

Made in the USA
Middletown, DE
09 November 2019